Verses of the Heart 2: A Poetic Journey Through Love's Whimsy

Heartstrings: Tales of Valentine's Verse, Volume 2

Said Al Azri

Published by Said Al Azri, 2024.

VERSES OF THE HEART 2: A POETIC JOURNEY THROUGH LOVE'S WHIMSY

First edition. January 8, 2024.

Copyright © 2024 Said Al Azri.

ISBN: 979-8224427826

Written by Said Al Azri.

Also by Said Al Azri

Heartstrings: Tales of Valentine's Verse
Verses of the Heart: A Poetic Journey Through Love's Whimsy
Verses of the Heart 2: A Poetic Journey Through Love's Whimsy

Living Fully After 50 Series
Rediscovering Hobbies and Passions After 50
Rediscovering Hobbies and Passions After 50, Book 2

Table of Contents

To my dearest Maida,

In every verse of this book, there echoes the melody of your love and support. You are the inspiration that dances through these pages, the unwavering beacon that lights my path. Your love, as deep and vast as the ocean, is the essence that breathes life into my words.

To our cherished children,

You are the living verses of our love story, the joyful symphony of our hearts. Your laughter is the music, and your dreams are the rhythm that guides my pen. In your eyes, I see the wonder of life; in your spirit, the boundless possibilities of love.

This book is a celebration of the love and happiness you infuse into every moment. May it mirror the beauty and depth of the joy you have brought into my life.

Forever and always, with all my love, Said

Verses of the Heart, a Symphony Restart

With each new verse, our hearts' symphony anew,
In the rhythm of love, emotions dance true.
Each word, a note in love's endless score,
Singing of romance, deeper than ever before.
In this symphonic restart, love finds its art,
Verses of the heart, playing cupid's dart.

* <> * <> * <> *

The Poetic Journey Through Love's Whimsy Continues

Through whimsy's gate, our poetic journey strides,
With new words of love, where enchantment abides.
In every line, a whimsical tale of affection,
Crafting a mosaic of love's intricate connection.
This journey's path, with new verses in queue,
Continues in wonder, ever fresh, ever true.

* <> * <> * <> *

Living Valentine's Day with New Words of Romance and Charm

In the embrace of new words, Valentine's charm we find,
Each a treasure of romance, uniquely designed.
With charm and with poetry, love's tale we spin,
In every stanza, a new love story begins.
Embracing the day with verses so warm,
We celebrate love in its most charming form.

151. Charm

In love's spell, charm is the magic,
A delightful trait, not tragic.
In its allure, nothing static,
A quality enchanting, love's fabric.
Charm, in love's attic,
An appealing feature, love's magnetic.

152. Dreamy

In love's fantasy, dreamy is the haze,
A whimsical state, love's maze.
In its trance, hearts blaze,
A visionary feeling, love's phase.
Dreamy, in love's glaze,
An idealistic quality, love's gaze.

153. Eternal

In love's infinity, eternal is the time,
A never-ending rhythm, love's chime.
In its perpetuity, hearts climb,
A timeless love, in its prime.
Eternal, in love's rhyme,
An everlasting bond, love's mime.

154. Fascination

In love's interest, fascination is the lure,
A captivating charm, pure and sure.
In its intrigue, hearts secure,
A strong attraction, love's tour.
Fascination, in love's demure,
An engrossing allure, love's cure.

155. Glow

In love's radiance, glow is the light,

A warm luminescence, bright and right.

In its shine, hearts sight,

A glowing aura, love's height.

Glow, in love's night,

A shining presence, love's kite.

156. Happiness

In love's joy, happiness is the cheer,
A state of bliss, love's peer.
In its glee, hearts veer,
A contented feeling, love's gear.
Happiness, in love's sphere,
A delightful emotion, love's seer.

157. Intrigue

In love's mystery, intrigue is the puzzle,
A curious interest, love's tussle.
In its fascination, hearts hustle,
A captivating mystery, love's muscle.
Intrigue, in love's bustle,
An enthralling charm, love's rustle.

158. Journey

In love's path, journey is the way,
A passage of time, love's bay.
In its travel, hearts sway,
A voyage of love, in every fray.
Journey, in love's play,
An adventurous route, love's day.

159. Keepsake

In love's memory, keepsake is the token,
A symbol of love, not broken.
In its hold, words unspoken,
A cherished item, love's spoken.
Keepsake, in love's woken,
A tangible memory, love's oaken.

160. Lavish

In love's abundance, lavish is the gift,
A generous display, love's shift.
In its extravagance, hearts uplift,
A bountiful offering, love's rift.
Lavish, in love's thrift,
An opulent gesture, love's silt.

161. Magic

In love's enchantment, magic is the spell,
A supernatural charm, where hearts dwell.
In its wonder, stories tell,
A mystical allure, love's well.
Magic, in love's cell,
An extraordinary power, love's bell.

162. Nestle

In love's comfort, nestle is the snuggle,
A cozy embrace, love's juggle.
In its warmth, hearts smuggle,
A tender cuddle, love's huddle.
Nestle, in love's muddle,
A secure hold, love's puddle.

163. Opulence

In love's wealth, opulence is the richness,
A sumptuous quality, love's fitness.
In its luxury, no quickness,
A lavish lifestyle, love's witness.
Opulence, in love's thickness,
An affluent state, love's business.

164. Paradise

In love's utopia, paradise is the land,
A blissful place, love's hand.
In its beauty, hearts stand,
A heavenly space, love's band.
Paradise, in love's strand,
An idyllic setting, love's grand.

165. Quench

In love's thirst, quench is the satisfy,
A fulfillment of desire, love's ally.
In its relief, hearts comply,
A quelling of craving, love's sky.
Quench, in love's cry,
A satiation of need, love's tie.

166. Rapture

In love's ecstasy, rapture is the bliss,
A state of joy, love's kiss.
In its fervor, no amiss,
A passionate delight, love's abyss.
Rapture, in love's dismiss,
An intense pleasure, love's reminisce.

167. Spellbound

In love's charm, spellbound is the captivate,

A bewitching allure, love's estate.

In its trance, hearts relate,

A mesmerizing state, love's fate.

Spellbound, in love's gate,

An enchanted feeling, love's plate.

168. Twilight

In love's dusk, twilight is the glow,
A soft light, love's show.
In its dimness, feelings grow,
A transitional time, love's bow.
Twilight, in love's flow,
A serene moment, love's slow.

169. Unity

In love's harmony, unity is the bond,
A concord of hearts, fond.
In its togetherness, beyond,
A union of souls, love's wand.
Unity, in love's pond,
A cohesive blend, love's correspond.

170. Veneration

In love's reverence, veneration is the honor,
A deep respect, love's donor.
In its esteem, no goner,
A profound admiration, love's corner.
Veneration, in love's sonar,
An act of devotion, love's loner.

171. Whimsical

In love's play, whimsical is the fancy,
A capricious charm, love's prancy.
In its quirk, no chancy,
A fanciful spirit, love's dancey.
Whimsical, in love's glancy,
A playful delight, love's advancey.

172. Xanadu

In love's paradise, Xanadu is the dream,
A place of beauty, love's stream.
In its splendor, hearts beam,
A utopian realm, love's cream.
Xanadu, in love's theme,
An idyllic haven, love's supreme.

173. Yearning

In love's desire, yearning is the ache,
A longing deep, love's bake.
In its crave, hearts shake,
A fervent need, love's stake.
Yearning, in love's wake,
An intense longing, love's rake.

174. Zenith

In love's peak, zenith is the top,
A pinnacle high, love's crop.
In its summit, hearts hop,
A highest point, love's prop.
Zenith, in love's shop,
An apex of affection, love's stop.

175. Amorous

In love's flame, amorous is the burn,
A romantic passion, love's turn.
In its ardor, hearts yearn,
A loving desire, love's churn.
Amorous, in love's urn,
An affectionate warmth, love's learn.

176. Bewitched

In love's spell, bewitched is the charm,
A magical allure, love's arm.
In its enchantment, no harm,
A captivating spell, love's farm.
Bewitched, in love's alarm,
An entranced state, love's warm.

177. Captivate

In love's allure, captivate is the hold,
A mesmerizing power, bold.
In its fascination, hearts are sold,
A compelling attraction, love's mold.
Captivate, in love's fold,
An irresistible charm, love's gold.

178. Dazzle

In love's brilliance, dazzle is the shine,
A stunning display, love's line.
In its splendor, hearts entwine,
A breathtaking effect, love's vine.
Dazzle, in love's pine,
An impressive radiance, love's sign.

179. Enthral

In love's grip, enthral is the captivate,
A spellbinding allure, love's state.
In its hold, hearts relate,
A fascinating charm, love's gate.
Enthral, in love's slate,
An absorbing attraction, love's mate.

180. Fond

In love's liking, fond is the affection,
A tender feeling, love's direction.
In its warmth, no objection,
A gentle fondness, love's section.
Fond, in love's collection,
A heartfelt attachment, love's reflection.

181. Gleam

In love's light, gleam is the spark,
A glint of affection, in the dark.
In its shimmer, hearts embark,
A bright flash, love's landmark.
Gleam, in love's arc,
A radiant shine, love's hallmark.

182. Honeysuckle

In love's garden, honeysuckle is the sweet,
A fragrant bloom, love's greet.
In its nectar, hearts meet,
A symbol of devotion, love's feat.
Honeysuckle, in love's seat,
A delicate allure, love's treat.

183. Illumine

In love's brightness, illumine is the light,
A glowing radiance, love's sight.
In its clarity, hearts ignite,
A luminous beam, love's kite.
Illumine, in love's night,
An enlightening glow, love's height.

184. Jubilee

In love's celebration, jubilee is the joy,
A festive occasion, love's toy.
In its merriment, no coy,
A grand celebration, love's ploy.
Jubilee, in love's employ,
A jubilant event, love's alloy.

185. Knighthood

In love's honor, knighthood is the valor,
A noble stature, love's parlor.
In its chivalry, no paler,
A gallant spirit, love's sailor.
Knighthood, in love's calor,
A distinguished courage, love's alor.

186. Lustrous

In love's gleam, lustrous is the shine,
A brilliant radiance, love's line.
In its gloss, hearts entwine,
A shimmering light, love's spine.
Lustrous, in love's pine,
A sparkling brightness, love's sign.

187. Mystical

In love's mystery, mystical is the charm,
A magical aura, love's arm.
In its enigma, no alarm,
A supernatural allure, love's farm.
Mystical, in love's swarm,
An otherworldly appeal, love's warm.

188. Nectarine

In love's fruit, nectarine is the sweet,
A juicy delight, love's treat.
In its succulence, hearts beat,
A symbol of freshness, love's seat.
Nectarine, in love's feat,
A tasty affection, love's greet.

189. Oblige

In love's duty, oblige is the bind,
A moral obligation, love's find.
In its commitment, hearts aligned,
A willing service, love's kind.
Oblige, in love's mind,
A compelled devotion, love's signed.

190. Passionflower

In love's flora, passionflower is the bloom,
A symbol of desire, in love's room.
In its beauty, hearts zoom,
A representation of ardor, love's loom.
Passionflower, in love's gloom,
An exotic emblem, love's boom.

191. Quaintly

In love's charm, quaintly is the grace,
A charming quality, love's embrace.
In its allure, a gentle pace,
A delightful quaintness, love's face.
Quaintly, in love's race,
An attractively old-fashioned love, love's base.

192. Rhapsody

In love's melody, rhapsody is the song,
A passionate tune, love's strong.
In its rhythm, hearts belong,
A lyrical ecstasy, love's throng.
Rhapsody, in love's long,
An emotional overture, love's gong.

193. Symphony

In love's orchestra, symphony is the sound,
A harmonious blend, love's round.
In its composition, feelings abound,
A majestic arrangement, love's ground.
Symphony, in love's mound,
An intricate concert, love's bound.

194. Tendril

In love's vine, tendril is the curl,
A spiraling growth, love's whirl.
In its reach, hearts unfurl,
A clinging embrace, love's pearl.
Tendril, in love's swirl,
A delicate twist, love's twirl.

195. Uplift

In love's support, uplift is the rise,
A boosting force, love's prize.
In its elevation, spirits apprise,
A lifting up, love's size.
Uplift, in love's ties,
An encouraging lift, love's highs.

196. Vibrant

In love's energy, vibrant is the zest,
A lively vigor, love's best.
In its vitality, hearts attest,
A dynamic aura, love's quest.
Vibrant, in love's chest,
A spirited enthusiasm, love's fest.

197. Wonder

In love's awe, wonder is the amaze,
A feeling of marvel, love's blaze.
In its astonishment, hearts gaze,
A profound admiration, love's phase.
Wonder, in love's maze,
An overwhelming fascination, love's daze.

198. Xenia

In love's hospitality, xenia is the guest,
A welcoming spirit, love's nest.
In its generosity, hearts attest,
A friendly reception, love's zest.
Xenia, in love's chest,
An ancient virtue, love's quest.

199. Yuletide

In love's holiday, Yuletide is the cheer,
A festive season, love's near.
In its celebration, hearts revere,
A time of joy, love's peer.
Yuletide, in love's leer,
A Christmas tradition, love's seer.

200. Zealous

In love's fervor, zealous is the fire,
A passionate intensity, love's wire.
In its ardor, hearts aspire,
A zealous enthusiasm, love's choir.
Zealous, in love's attire,
An intense devotion, love's spire.

201. Beloved

In love's heart, beloved is the dear,
A cherished person, love's steer.
In its affection, hearts reappear,
A loved one, love's gear.
Beloved, in love's leer,
An adored individual, love's peer.

202. Cherished

In love's embrace, cherished is the treasure,
A valued being, love's measure.
In its esteem, hearts pleasure,
A precious entity, love's leisure.
Cherished, in love's seizure,
A dearly held person, love's feature.

203. Dream

In love's vision, dream is the wish,
A hopeful fantasy, love's dish.
In its slumber, hearts swish,
A whimsical thought, love's fish.
Dream, in love's dish,
An imaginative reverie, love's quish.

204. Elegy

In love's mourning, elegy is the song,
A sorrowful ode, love's long.
In its lament, hearts throng,
A mournful poem, love's prong.
Elegy, in love's bong,
An expression of grief, love's tong.

205. Fervor

In love's intensity, fervor is the heat,
A passionate zeal, love's beat.
In its ardor, hearts fleet,
A fervent spirit, love's seat.
Fervor, in love's treat,
An enthusiastic flame, love's greet.

206. Gaiety

In love's joy, gaiety is the cheer,
A lively merriment, love's beer.
In its festivity, hearts leer,
A playful happiness, love's peer.
Gaiety, in love's steer,
An exuberant delight, love's rear.

207. Heartland

In love's core, heartland is the center,
A foundational love, love's enter.
In its essence, hearts mentor,
A central feeling, love's venter.
Heartland, in love's renter,
An emotional hub, love's epicenter.

208. Idolize

In love's adoration, idolize is the worship,
A profound reverence, love's ship.
In its admiration, hearts flip,
A devoted esteem, love's grip.
Idolize, in love's dip,
An intense veneration, love's clip.

209. Jasmine

In love's flora, jasmine is the scent,
A fragrant blossom, love's rent.
In its aroma, hearts bent,
A sweet-smelling flower, love's tent.
Jasmine, in love's lent,
An aromatic bloom, love's event.

210. Kindle

In love's ignition, kindle is the spark,
A firestarter, love's mark.
In its flame, hearts embark,
A warming blaze, love's lark.
Kindle, in love's park,
An initiating fire, love's stark.

211. Lullaby

In love's song, lullaby is the tune,
A soothing melody, love's rune.
In its rhythm, hearts swoon,
A calming chant, love's boon.
Lullaby, in love's cocoon,
A gentle hymn, love's moon.

212. Majestic

In love's grandeur, majestic is the splendor,
A royal magnificence, love's vendor.
In its awe, hearts render,
A magnificent presence, love's tender.
Majestic, in love's blender,
An imposing beauty, love's sender.

213. Nuzzle

In love's caress, nuzzle is the rub,
A tender touch, love's hub.
In its closeness, hearts sub,
A gentle snuggle, love's club.
Nuzzle, in love's shrub,
An affectionate gesture, love's grub.

214. Overjoyed

In love's elation, overjoyed is the leap,
A bound of happiness, love's deep.
In its thrill, hearts keep,
A jubilant jump, love's steep.
Overjoyed, in love's heap,
An ecstatic joy, love's reap.

215. Pristine

In love's purity, pristine is the clear,
A flawless state, love's dear.
In its cleanliness, hearts cheer,
An unblemished love, love's sphere.
Pristine, in love's gear,
An immaculate affection, love's peer.

216. Quintessence

In love's essence, quintessence is the core,
A perfect example, love's lore.
In its epitome, hearts soar,
The ultimate instance, love's oar.
Quintessence, in love's store,
An ideal exemplar, love's door.

217. Romanticize

In love's ideal, romanticize is the dream,
A fanciful view, love's stream.
In its embellishment, hearts gleam,
A beautified love, love's beam.
Romanticize, in love's scheme,
An imaginative notion, love's seam.

218. Sapphire

In love's gem, sapphire is the blue,
A radiant jewel, love's clue.
In its brilliance, hearts true,
A precious stone, love's view.
Sapphire, in love's stew,
A symbol of loyalty, love's due.

219. Tactile

In love's touch, tactile is the feel,
A physical contact, love's keel.
In its sensation, hearts deal,
A tangible affection, love's wheel.
Tactile, in love's zeal,
An intimate touch, love's seal.

220. Undying

In love's eternity, undying is the forever,
A ceaseless devotion, love's endeavor.
In its perpetuity, hearts sever,
An endless love, love's lever.
Undying, in love's never,
An immortal love, love's ever.

221. Velour

In love's texture, velour is the velvet,
A soft fabric, love's helmet.
In its smoothness, hearts melt,
A plush feel, love's pelt.
Velour, in love's welt,
A luxurious touch, love's felt.

222. Wanderlust

In love's adventure, wanderlust is the yearn,
A desire to explore, love's turn.
In its craving, hearts burn,
A travel lust, love's churn.
Wanderlust, in love's urn,
An urge to roam, love's adjourn.

223. Xenial

In love's hospitality, xenial is the welcome,
A friendly reception, love's outcome.
In its warmth, hearts become,
An amiable greeting, love's succumb.
Xenial, in love's drum,
A hospitable nature, love's hum.

224. Youthful

In love's vigor, youthful is the spry,
A lively energy, love's sky.
In its freshness, hearts fly,
A youthful spirit, love's tie.
Youthful, in love's cry,
An exuberant zest, love's ally.

225. Zestful

In love's vibrancy, zestful is the spark,
A lively enthusiasm, love's arc.
In its zest, hearts embark,
A spirited fervor, love's mark.
Zestful, in love's lark,
An energetic passion, love's park.

226. Adulation

In love's praise, adulation is the song,
A fervent admiration, love's gong.
In its acclaim, hearts long,
A deep reverence, love's strong.
Adulation, in love's throng,
An enthusiastic esteem, love's prolong.

227. Bequest

In love's gift, bequest is the legacy,
A cherished endowment, love's elegy.
In its inheritance, hearts agree,
A lasting token, love's spree.
Bequest, in love's decree,
An enduring present, love's key.

228. Cinnamon

In love's spice, cinnamon is the scent,
A warm aroma, love's ascent.
In its flavor, hearts relent,
A sweet spice, love's intent.
Cinnamon, in love's tent,
An aromatic delight, love's event.

229. Dewdrop

In love's morning, dewdrop is the jewel,
A glistening bead, love's fuel.
In its freshness, hearts rule,
A tiny droplet, love's pool.
Dewdrop, in love's cool,
A symbol of newness, love's tool.

230. Ebullient

In love's cheer, ebullient is the burst,
A joyful exuberance, love's thirst.
In its bubbling, hearts first,
A lively excitement, love's nursed.
Ebullient, in love's versed,
An effervescent spirit, love's immersed.

231. Felicity

In love's happiness, felicity is the bliss,
A profound joy, love's kiss.
In its contentment, hearts reminisce,
A state of happiness, love's abyss.
Felicity, in love's hiss,
An intense happiness, love's miss.

232. Garnet

In love's gem, garnet is the stone,
A deep red crystal, love's own.
In its hue, hearts are shown,
A symbol of love, love's known.
Garnet, in love's zone,
A precious gem, love's throne.

233. Hibiscus

In love's flora, hibiscus is the bloom,

A tropical flower, love's room.

In its beauty, hearts groom,

A vibrant blossom, love's loom.

Hibiscus, in love's boom,

An exotic presence, love's doom.

234. Iridescent

In love's color, iridescent is the shine,
A rainbow sheen, love's line.
In its spectrum, hearts entwine,
A colorful radiance, love's spine.
Iridescent, in love's vine,
A shimmering glow, love's sign.

235. Joviality

In love's fun, joviality is the laughter,
A cheerful spirit, love's hereafter.
In its mirth, hearts raft,
A joyous mood, love's craft.
Joviality, in love's shaft,
An amusing delight, love's draft.

236. Knell

In love's farewell, knell is the toll,
A solemn ringing, love's bowl.
In its sound, hearts patrol,
A bell of ending, love's role.
Knell, in love's stole,
A signaling chime, love's coal.

237. Lilac

In love's bloom, lilac is the scent,
A fragrant whisper, love's ascent.
In its hues, hearts relent,
A soft color, love's content.
Lilac, in love's tent,
A symbol of first emotions, love's advent.

238. Marigold

In love's garden, marigold is the sun,
A bright blossom, love's spun.
In its glow, hearts won,
A cheerful flower, love's fun.
Marigold, in love's run,
A symbol of light, love's begun.

239. Nightingale

In love's song, nightingale is the voice,
A melodious call, love's choice.
In its tune, hearts rejoice,
A serenade of nature, love's poise.
Nightingale, in love's noise,
A symbol of passion, love's joys.

240. Overture

In love's prelude, overture is the start,
A musical beginning, love's art.
In its symphony, hearts part,
An introduction to love, love's heart.
Overture, in love's chart,
A grand opening, love's smart.

241. Peony

In love's display, peony is the bloom,
A lush flower, love's room.
In its fullness, hearts groom,
A symbol of wealth, love's loom.
Peony, in love's tomb,
A lush and luxurious flower, love's boom.

242. Quixotic Love

In love's dream, quixotic love is the ideal,
A romantic fantasy, love's zeal.
In its pursuit, hearts feel,
An unrealistic quest, love's wheel.
Quixotic love, in love's keel,
A fanciful journey, love's seal.

243. Rosebud

In love's promise, rosebud is the start,
A symbol of newness, love's heart.
In its bloom, hearts dart,
A budding love, love's chart.
Rosebud, in love's mart,
A sign of young love, love's part.

244. Stargazer

In love's sky, stargazer is the dreamer,
A celestial admirer, love's screamer.
In its gaze, hearts gleam,
An upward look, love's beam.
Stargazer, in love's stream,
A dreamy soul, love's theme.

245. Tulip

In love's gesture, tulip is the gift,
A colorful offering, love's lift.
In its elegance, hearts shift,
A symbol of perfect love, love's miff.
Tulip, in love's rift,
A beautiful token, love's thrift.

246. Umbrella

In love's shelter, umbrella is the cover,
A protective canopy, love's lover.
In its embrace, hearts hover,
A shared space, love's discover.
Umbrella, in love's over,
A cozy haven, love's rover.

247. Vanilla

In love's flavor, vanilla is the sweet,
A classic essence, love's meet.
In its scent, hearts beat,
A comforting aroma, love's greet.
Vanilla, in love's fleet,
A familiar and warm scent, love's treat.

248. Wisteria

In love's cascade, wisteria is the fall,
A flowing bloom, love's call.
In its drapes, hearts stall,
A symbol of romance, love's hall.
Wisteria, in love's mall,
A graceful flower, love's pall.

249. XOXO Hugs

In love's signature, XOXO hugs are the mark,
A symbol of affection, love's spark.
In its embrace, hearts embark,
A playful gesture, love's park.
XOXO hugs, in love's dark,
A sign of love and warmth, love's lark.

250. Ylang-Ylang

In love's aroma, Ylang-Ylang is the scent,
An exotic fragrance, love's bent.
In its perfume, hearts are sent,
A sensual aroma, love's rent.
Ylang-Ylang, in love's tent,
A deeply floral fragrance, love's extent.

Don't miss out!

Visit the website below and you can sign up to receive emails whenever Said Al Azri publishes a new book. There's no charge and no obligation.

https://books2read.com/r/B-A-KSLCB-NHFTC

BOOKS2READ

Connecting independent readers to independent writers.

Also by Said Al Azri

Heartstrings: Tales of Valentine's Verse
Verses of the Heart: A Poetic Journey Through Love's Whimsy
Verses of the Heart 2: A Poetic Journey Through Love's Whimsy

Living Fully After 50 Series
Rediscovering Hobbies and Passions After 50
Rediscovering Hobbies and Passions After 50, Book 2